© Copyright 2015

Written by Sally A Jones and Amanda C Jones
Illustrations by Annalisa Jones

Published by GUINEA PIG EDUCATION

2 Cobs Way,
New Haw,
Addlestone,
Surrey,
KT15 3AF.
www.guineapigeducation.co.uk

NO part of this publication may be reproduced, stored or copied for commercial purposes and profit without the prior written permission of the publishers.

ISBN: 9781910824009

Use this book if you speak English as a foreign language and you want to improve your writing skills in English and increase your vocabulary, so you can write letters, emails and articles in everyday life.

To grasp better English, you will need to know the material on the following pages.

Here is an example:

> Zoggy has lost his notebook. He goes over his movements of the previous day, but a thorough search, of his space craft, does not bring it to light. He wonders where it is.

This version is easier to understand.

> Zoggy has lost his notebook. He goes over (in his mind) all the places he went to on the previous day, but a thorough search, of his spacecraft, does not help him find it. "Where can it be," he thinks.

Have you ever been baffled by words or phrases used in the English language? Were you unable to make head or tail (*idiom for no understanding*) **of what was being said?**

The following pages will help you get the hang of (*used to*) informal English, so you will never get into hot water (*get into difficulty*) speaking English words. You will never rub anyone up the wrong way (*antagonise anyone with the words you say*), or put your foot in it (*say something out of place*).

Now, find out what it all means:

The trouble and strife
Cockney rhyming slang for wife.

A bit steep
Too much money

Daylight robbery
Extortionate price

Keep your hair on
Stop being so angry.

Never look a gift horse in the mouth
Be happy with the discount

A cheap skate
A mean, miserly person

Where's the apple and pears
Cockney rhyming slang for stairs.

Humming and harring
Can't decide which one to get.

Having a laugh
You must be fooling me

Get your knickers in a twist
Don't get angry or annoyed

A rip off
Too expensive

Just cough up
Pay the money

Costs an arm and a leg
Unreasonable price

Zoggy wonders what it really means.
Match to the one you think is right.

I got <u>carried away</u> shopping.	not my usual self.
I found my work hard, but my friend was <u>in the same boat</u>.	cause embarrassment by something you say or do.
This month I am <u>hard up</u>.	put on a good outward show
On the weekend, I was at <u>a loose end</u>.	badly affected
My friend is <u>a good for nothing</u>.	I was so excited I bought too much.
I am <u>off form</u>.	lazy
I have been <u>hard hit</u> by these circumstances.	meet the circumstances head on.
I really <u>put my foot in it</u>.	crazy about a particular idea.
I am <u>at loggerheads</u> with my boss.	ignored me
She gave me <u>the cold shoulder</u>.	make a fresh start
I have to <u>face the music</u>.	short of cash
She tries to <u>keep up appearances</u>.	over doing work and having little sleep
She had a <u>bee in her bonnet</u>.	in the same position
I have been <u>burning the candle at both ends</u>.	have quarrelled.
I would advise you to <u>make a clean break of it</u>.	had nothing to do

I feel <u>out of sorts</u> this morning.	a snobbish, conceited person
He does not <u>come up to the mark</u>.	going through a time of suffering
I <u>sent him packing.</u>	an extremely well loved person.
He is a <u>chip off the old block</u>.	a son is like his Dad.
She is <u>stuck up</u>.	feel unwell
She has <u>turned over a new leaf</u>.	to take days off work without permission.
My nephew is the <u>apple of my eye</u>.	out of my mind with worry
My friend is <u>going through the mill</u>.	is dead
He is <u>over the hill.</u>	get rid of quickly.
I am <u>beside myself</u>.	got into trouble
He was only <u>pulling your leg</u>.	reached the required standard
If he wanted me to help, he shouldn't have <u>rubbed me up the wrong way</u>.	made me desire to eat it.
That cake made my <u>mouth water</u>.	teasing you
Alfie is <u>at rest</u> now.	make a fresh start
I got into <u>hot water</u>.	annoyed me
I will take <u>French leave</u>.	too old

I am going to sit on the fence.	to not get to the point
I threw cold water on it.	to accomplish two things at once
She is playing with fire.	I won't worry about it until it happens
I am going to take forty winks.	very expensive
He got on his high horse.	not very well
Please don't rub it in.	not take sides
He is beating round the bush.	don't panic
I took on more than I could chew.	when you've failed at a task, it is time to start over again
I'll cross that bridge when I come to it.	discourage someone from carrying out an idea
Keep your hair on.	missed your chance/ opportunity
Back to the drawing board.	monopolising conversation
It cost an arm and a leg.	have a nap
Don't give up your day job.	to go to bed
I'm feeling a bit under the weather.	involved in something controversial
I'll give him the benefit of the doubt.	go over and over something, to make the listener jealous
I'm going to hit the sack.	more than I could cope with
I'll kill two birds with one stone.	you are not very good at something
I really missed the boat.	to believe someone without proof.

It's a piece of cake.	do not agree on an issue
I wouldn't be caught dead doing that.	to take the simplest or cheapest option and, as such, do the job badly.
We don't see eye to eye.	you got what you deserve.
I go there once in a blue moon.	to come to the point succinctly
She is really on the ball.	heard rumours about that
Speak of the devil.	really easy
It's a taste of your own medicine.	there are only advantages
Your guess is as good as mine.	joined a popular trend
She's pulled the wool over their eyes.	clued up/ understands what is going on.
To make a long story short.	very rarely
He's jumped on the bandwagon.	do it in an instant
I heard that on the grapevine.	understand it
It's a blessing in disguise.	looking in the wrong place
They have really cut corners.	I would never do that
They are barking up the wrong tree.	you are talking about someone, when by coincidence they appear.
I would go at the drop of a hat.	no point worrying about something in the past which you can not change
It is the best of both worlds.	something that turns out to be good, but is not recognised at first.
Don't cry over spilt milk.	to deceive someone
I could not make head or tail of it.	to have no idea about something.

Make sure you know these similes which are in common use.

Similes *compare* using 'like' or 'as'

Match the similes

as light	as a feather
as poor	as thieves
as fit	as a bone
as free	as a ghost
as right	as an owl
as wise	as a fiddle
as thick	as punch
as safe	as rain
as white	as a mouse
as bright	as coal
as black	as a button
as big	as two peas in a pod
as alike	as ice
as cold	as an elephant
as pleased	as silk
as smooth	as a rake
as thin	as a bird
as quiet	as an eel
as slippery	as houses
as dry	as a church mouse

(as light → as a feather; as thick → as thieves; as thin → as a rake shown by arrows)

These similes are well known sayings but you can make up some of your own.

For example:

Look after the pennies and the pounds will look after themselves. ⟶ means ⟶ Be careful how you spend you money.

PROVERB	MEANING
A bad workman blames his tools.	
Make hay while the sun shines.	
Every cloud has a silver lining.	
Let sleeping dogs lie.	
You've made your bed, now lie in it.	
A friend in need is a friend indeed.	
Absence makes the heart grow fonder.	
First come, first served.	
One good turn deserves another.	
A new broom sweeps clean.	
No news is good news.	
Great minds think alike.	
A bird in the hand is worth two in the bush.	
Never judge a book by its cover.	
A leopard does not change its spots.	
A little of what you fancy does you good.	
A problem shared is a problem halved.	
Many hands make light work.	
Actions speak louder than words.	
Practice what you preach.	

PROVERB	MEANING
All good things come to he who waits.	
All that glitters is not gold.	
What doesn't kill us makes us stronger.	
Count your blessings.	
It takes one to know one.	
As thick as thieves.	
Be careful what you wish for.	
Beauty is only skin deep.	
Beggars cannot be choosers.	
Better late than never.	
Better to have loved and lost than never to have loved at all.	
Blood is thicker than water.	
An apple a day keeps the doctor away.	
Don't put all your eggs in one basket.	
No rest for the wicked.	
There's no smoke without fire.	
Don't try to run before you can walk.	
Enough is enough.	
First come, first serve.	
First things first.	

PROVERB	MEANING
Every picture tells a story.	
Flattery will get you nowhere.	
Fools rush in where angels fear to tread.	
Give a man enough rope and he will hang himself.	
Give credit where credit is due.	
Go the extra mile.	
He who laughs last, laughs longest.	
If you can't beat them, join them.	
Marry in haste, repent at leisure.	
Wonders will never cease.	
The fruit does not fall far from the tree.	
Money doesn't grow on trees.	
You reap what you sow.	
The grass is always greener on the other side of the fence.	
Too many cooks spoil the broth.	
Lightning never strikes the same place twice.	
It goes without saying.	
Honesty is the best policy.	
If the cap fits, wear it.	
Pride comes before a fall.	

Make sure you know these group terms.

an army of soldiers	a band of musicians	a class of scholars
a company of actors	a drove of cattle	a flock of sheep
a gaggle of geese	a herd of cattle	a litter of pups
a pack of wolves	a plague of insects	a pride of lions
a shoal of herring	a swarm of bees	a troupe of dancers
a bouquet of flowers	a bunch of grapes	a pack of cards
a fleet of cars	a string of beads	a galaxy of stars
a peal of bells	a bunch of bananas	a library of books

You will find:

an audience at a concert.	a spectator at the match.
a congregation in the church.	a crowd in the street.

Make sure you know these sounds made by objects.

bang of a door	clanking of chains	crack of a whip.
blast of an explosion	the patter of feet	howling of the wind
gurgle of the stream	screeching of brakes	singing of the kettle
thunder of hoofs	tinkle of glass	roar of a torrent
rumble of a train	the rustle of leaves	sighing of the wind
swish of skirts	wail of a siren	popping of corks

Make sure you know these gender words.

bachelor or spinster	hero or heroine	nephew or niece
uncle or aunt	dog or bitch	stallion or mare
boar or sow	cock or hen	colt or filly

Make sure you know these family words.

lion lioness cub	bull cow calf
ram yew lamb	gander goose gosling

"Feeling baffled? Find out what they mean."

Know these popular phrases.

as the crow flies	pins and needles	a fine kettle of fish
a stiff upper lip	a storm in a teacup	with flying colours
horse play	a birds eye view	cock and bull story

Make sure you know these doubles.

His business went to rack and ruin.	The child was found safe and sound.
She kept her house spick and span.	He was at his bosses beck and call.
They argued hammer and tongs.	We searched high and low.
They went through ups and downs in their relationship.	The customer was ranting and raving at the till.

Make sure you know these colour words.

He was the black sheep of the family.	I saw it in black and white.
It was a red letter day.	The production was a white elephant.
He has green eye.	He has the blues.

Jot down any more proverbs, idioms or similes you come across here.

BE AWARE OF THOSE LITTLE WORDS THAT FOLLOW VERBS CALLED PREPOSITIONS IN ENGLISH.

Be aware of the correct prepositions in English grammar.

"Sometimes words have special prepositions that always accompany them."

Finish the sentences, putting in the correct prepositions.

1. I am ashamed **of** the way my brother behaved in class.

2. I took the blame **for** the broken vase.

3. I will not comment **on** my appalling exam results.

4. Compared .... my friend, I excelled at history.

5. I was conscious .... a ghostly presence in the room.

6. I disagree .... the changes made by the new headteacher.

7. I was disappointed .... my teams performance.

8. I am disgusted .... people who drop litter in the street.

9. He was guilty .... a terrible crime.

10. I live opposite .... Mr. Smith.

11. He looks similar .... my dad.

12. She suffers .... a rare condition.

13. I will write .... my German friend.

14. I will eagerly wait .... some more news.

Many people learning to write in English get these wrong.

Get someone to test you.

1. angry with angry at	2. complain to	3. according to
4. similar to	5. blame for	6. change for
7. agree with	8. divide between divide among	9. comment on
10. aim for aim at	11. regard for	12. ashamed of
13. inspired by	14. protest against	15. attack on
16. compare with	17. opposite of	18. filled with
19. conscious of	20. pursuit of	21. full of
22. dislike for	23. rely on	24. die of
25. victim of	26. filled with	27. differ from
28. indignant at	29. disgusted with disgusted at	30. equal to
31. suffer from	32. guilty of	33. despair of
34. good for	35. wait for wait upon	36. thirst for
37. disagree with	38. disappointed in disappointed with	39. write to write about
40. tired of tired with	41. defiance of	42. protest against

CHECK YOUR ANSWERS

Page 8

I got carried away shopping - I was so excited I bought too much
I found my work hard, but my friend was in the same boat - in the same position
This month I am hard up - short of cash
On the weekend, I was at a loose end - had nothing to do
My friend is a good for nothing - lazy
I am off form - not my usual self
I have been hard hit by these circumstances - badly affected
I really put my foot in it - cause embarrassment by something you say or do.
I am at loggerheads with my boss - have quarrelled
She gave me the cold shoulder - ignored me
I have to face the music - meet the circumstances head on
She tries to keep up appearances - put on a good outward show
She had a bee in her bonnet - crazy about a particular idea
I have been burning the candle at both ends - over doing work and having little sleep
I would advise you to make a clean break of it - make a fresh start

Page 9

I feel out of sorts this morning - feel unwell
He does not come up to the mark - reached the required standard
I sent him packing - get rid of quickly
He is a chip off the old block - a son is like his Dad
She is stuck up - a snobbish, conceited person
She has turned over a new leaf - made a fresh start
My nephew is the apple of my eye - an extremely well loved person
My friend is going through the mill - going through a time of suffering
He is over the hill - too old
I am beside myself - out of my mind with worry
He was only pulling your leg - teasing you
If he wanted me to help, he shouldn't have rubbed me up the wrong way - annoyed me
That cake made my mouth water - made me desire to eat it
Alfie is at rest now - is dead
I got into hot water - got into trouble
I will take French leave - to take days off work without permission

Page 10

I am going to sit on the fence - not take sides
I threw cold water on it - discourage someone from carrying out an idea
She is playing with fire - involved in something controversial
I am going to take forty winks - have a nap
He got on his high horse - monopolising the conversation
Please don't rub it in - go over and over something, to make the listener jealous
He is beating round the bush - to not get to the point
I took on more than I could chew - more than I could cope with
I'll cross that bridge when I come to it - I won't worry about it until it happens
Keep your hair on - don't panic
Back to the drawing board - when you've failed at a task, it is time to start over again
It cost an arm and a leg - very expensive
Don't give up your day job - you are not very good at something
I'm feeling a bit under the weather - not very well
I'll give him the benefit of the doubt - to believe someone without proof
I'm going to hit the sack - go to bed
I'll kill two birds with one stone - to accomplish two things at once
I really missed the boat - missed your chance/opportunity

Page 11

It's a piece of cake - really easy
I wouldn't be caught dead doing that - I would never do that
We don't see eye to eye - do not agree on an issue
I go there once in a blue moon - very rarely
She is really on the ball - clued up/ understands what is going on

CHECK YOUR ANSWERS

Speak of the devil - you are talking about someone, when by coincidence they appear
It's a taste of your own medicine - you got what you deserve
Your guess is as good as mine - to have no idea about something
She's pulled the wool over their eyes - to deceive someone
To make a long story short - to come to the point succinctly
He's jumped on the bandwagon - joined a popular trend
I heard that on the grapevine - heard rumours about that
It's a blessing in disguise - something that turns out to be good, but is not recognised at first.
They have really cut corners - to take the simplest or cheapest option and, as such, do the job badly.
They are barking up the wrong tree - looking in the wrong place
I would go at the drop of a hat - do it in an instant
It is the best of both worlds - there are only advantages
Don't cry over spilt milk - no point worrying about something in the past which you can not change
I could not make head or tail of it - understand it

Page 12

as light as a feather	as poor as a church mouse	as fit as a fiddle	as free as a bird
as right as rain	as wise as an owl	as thick as thieves	as safe as houses
as alike as two peas in a pod	as cold as ice	as pleased as punch	as smooth as silk
as thin as a rake	as quiet as a mouse	as slippery as an eel	as dry as a bone
as white as a ghost	as bright as a button	as black as coal	as big as an elephant

Page 14

A bad workman blames his tools - to cover up your own shortcomings by making excuses
Make hay while the sun shines - make the most of a good opportunity while it lasts
Every cloud has a silver lining - there are advantages to be found in every bad situation
Let sleeping dogs lie - you shouldn't bring up a bad situation that everyone has forgotten about
You've made your bed, now lie in it - you have to put up with the consequences of your actions
A friend in need is a friend indeed - a friend who helps you in your time of need, is a true friend
Absence makes the heart grow fonder - when we are separated from the people we love, we love them more
First come, first served - people will be dealt with in the order in which they arrive
One good turn deserves another - you should pay back a good turn done for you, by doing a good turn for someone else
A new broom sweeps clean - for example, in a workplace if there is a change in management, many changes are likely to follow
No news is good news - if something bad had happened, you would have heard about it
Great minds think alike - said when two people come to the same conclusion or have the same idea at the same time
A bird in the hand is worth two in the bush - you should not jeopardise something you already have, by trying to get something better
Never judge a book by its cover - don't make judgements based on external appearances
A leopard does not change its spots - a person is unlikely to change their character, however hard they try
A problem shared is a problem halved - if you talk about a problem, you will feel better about it
Many hands make light work - if everyone helps with a task, the task will be accomplished faster
Actions speak louder than words - what you do is more important than what you say
Practice what you preach - take your own advice

Page 15

All good things come to he who waits - be patient and good things will happen to you
All that glitters is not gold - even if something looks good at a first glance/ outer appearances, it may not turn out to be good
What doesn't kill us makes us stronger - we are made stronger by the trials and tribulations that we go through in life
Count your blessings - be grateful for the good things you have in your life and don't dwell on the negative
It takes one to know one (it takes a thief to know a thief) - it takes a dishonest person to know what a dishonest person might do
Be careful what you wish for - if you get the thing you desire, there may be unforeseen consequences
Beauty is only skin deep - a persons character is more important than the way they look
Beggars cannot be choosers - you must accept an offer/situation, because there is no other choice
Better late than never - it is better for something to happen or someone to arrive late, than not to happen or come at all
Better to have loved and lost than never to have loved at all - better to have experienced a situation/event and lost it or it to have failed, than for it never to have happened at all

CHECK YOUR ANSWERS

Blood is thicker than water - relatives/ family should always come first
An apple a day keeps the doctor away - if you eat an apple every day, you will be healthy and not succumb to sickness, so will not need to see the doctor
Don't put all your eggs in one basket - but rather keep your options open
No rest for the wicked - religious imagery from the bible, referring to people as sinners and hence wicked, so deserving of no rest.
There's no smoke without fire - if bad things are said about someone or something, there is probably good reason for it
Don't try to run before you can walk - don't take on more than you can cope with
Enough is enough - you are so frustrated with something, that you want to to stop
First come first serve - deal with something promptly and you will be given priority (arrive first and you'll be served first)
First things first - start with the most important thing first

Page 17

Every picture tells a story - said when a situation looks exactly the way it is
Flattery will get you nowhere - flattering someone will not persuade them to do what you want them to do
Fools rush in where angels fear to tread - rash and inexperienced people attempt tasks without due care and attention
Give a man enough rope and he will hang himself - if you give a person freedom to do as he or she wants, eventually their behaviour will reveal his or her true character
Give credit where credit is due - you should praise someone if they deserve it
Go the extra mile - go out of your way to help or do something
He who laughs last, laughs longest - the last person to control a situation has the final say
If you can't beat them, join them - you recognise that you cannot be as successful as other people without doing what they do
Marry in haste, repent at leisure - if you marry someone too hastily, you may regret it when it is too late
Wonders will never cease - often said sarcastically, if something unusual or unexpected happens
The fruit does not fall far from the tree - a child is similar to their parent, shows the same (often bad) habits
Money doesn't grow on trees - money is not endlessly available
You reap what you sow - everything that happens to you is a result of your own actions and so your own fault
The grass is always greener on the other side of the fence - other people always seem to be in a better situation than you, even if they are not
Too many cooks spoil the broth - too many people working on a task, will be a hinderance not a help
Lightning never strikes the same place twice - bad things do not happen to the same person twice
It goes without saying - it doesn't need to be said, it is obvious that...
Honesty is the best policy - it is better to tell the truth than to lie
If the cap fits, wear it - you should be prepared to accept criticism and learn from it
Pride comes before a fall - don't be too arrogant in your abilities to do something or you may fail and will have a long way to fall

Page 20

1. I am ashamed of the way my brother behaved in class.
2. I took the blame for the broken vase.
3. I will not comment on my appalling exam results.
4. Compared to my friend, I excelled at history.
5. I was conscious of a ghostly presence in the room.
6. I disagree with the changes made by the new headteacher.
7. I was disappointed in my teams performance.
8. I am disgusted by people who drop litter in the street.
9. He was guilty of a terrible crime.
10. I live opposite to Mr. Smith.
11. He looks similar to my dad.
12. She suffers from a rare condition.
13. I will write to my German friend.
14. I will eagerly wait for some more news.

USE BETTER VOCABULARY.

This section helps you improve your vocabulary. It shows you how to move away from simple words (nice, said) and replace them with more interesting words.

ZOGGY'S JOURNAL

My experiences on earth...

Zoggy's letters, in this section, will show you how to set out a letter in English.

Let's peep into Zoggy's diary.

Zoggy visits the estate agent who writes down his requirements.

"I am looking for a **nice** house. I want a **nice** garden surrounding the property with **nice** flowers and **nice** fruit trees, which is big enough to grow a selection of vegetables.

I need a **nice** loft with a **nice** view of the sky from the window, that is suitable for a loft conversion. A **nice** garage is also required to store my sports car, so it doesn't attract too much attention.

Finally, the property must be **nice**. It must have **nice** bedrooms to entertain guests. It will need **nice** cupboards to store space equipment and specimens collected on earth."

"THIS HOUSE IS NOT INTERESTING AT ALL."

TASK

Can you make the description more interesting?
Replace the word 'nice' with other adjectives.

TAKE TWO
as they say in the film world.

"I am looking for an **impressive** house. I want an **extensive** garden surrounding the property with **fragrant** flowers and **luscious** fruit trees, which is big enough to grow a selection of vegetables.

I need a **spacious** loft which **commands an excellent** view of the sky from the window, that is suitable for a loft conversion. A **substantial** garage is also required to store my sports car, so it doesn't attract too much attention.

Finally, the property must be **well maintained**. It must have **airy** and **comfortable** bedrooms to entertain guests. It will need **vast** cupboards to store space equipment and specimens collected on earth."

THIS HOUSE SOUNDS GREAT!

Kitchen

Bedroom

I have moved in and am enjoying my new earth holiday home.

Zzzz...
Zzzz...
Zzzz...

HELLO!

RIDICULOUS!

Fill in the gaps with more advanced vocabulary. Use the words and phrases on the previous page to help you.

My house ...*has got*... several spacious rooms. The bedroom has .... a super king size bed and a walk in wardrobe, whilst the lounge .... a luxurious three piece suite, a coffee table and a T.V mounted on the wall.

The house .... central heating and running water. Moreover, it .... primitive technology; a landline phone, a computer, broadband internet and a home entertainment system.

Zoggy shakes his head in disbelief. He concludes that there is much he could teach earthlings.

The house ...*has not got*... any robots to do the housework; ...*it has got*... a fridge, a washing machine, a freezer and a hazardous looking microwave oven. He is not sure how to use these devices.

It has not .... the latest intergalactic computer system 'Solar net', to communicate with worlds deep into outer space.

"Annoying! I feel isolated from my own lands," Zoggy says.

20th Century Earth Mobile

Check your answers.

My house **consists of** several spacious rooms. The bedroom has **been fitted with** a super king size bed and a walk in wardrobe, whilst the lounge **is furnished with** a luxurious three piece suite, a coffee table and a T.V mounted on the wall.

The house **is installed with** central heating and running water. Moreover, it **is crammed full of** primitive technology: a landline phone, a computer, broadband internet, and a home entertainment system.

Zoggy shakes his head in disbelief. He concludes that there is much he could teach earthlings.

The house **lacks** any robots to do the housework, **with the exception of** a fridge, a washing machine, a freezer and a hazardous looking microwave oven. He is not sure how to use these devices.

It has not **acquired** the latest intergalactic computer system 'Solar net', to communicate with worlds deep into outer space.

"Annoying! I feel isolated from my own lands," Zoggy grumbles.

FIRST VISITOR

A hungry mouse **looks** out of a hole. The **noise** of my snores **tells** him that I am **fast** asleep in my chair. The **leftover** lunch **is** on the kitchen table and he **starts** to **eat** the **nice scraps of food**. I **open** one eye sleepily. I stretch, yawn and stand up.

The mouse is a ………………………………… earth phenomenon I have never …………………………… before? I ……………… my notebook to record my findings.

I …………………… a thorough ……………………, but it is too late because the little creature ………………………… to safety. I………… to my …………………… chair.

A mouse

Check your answers.

A hungry mouse **peers** out of the hole. The **sound** of my snores **informs** him that I am **deeply** asleep in my chair. The **remains** of my lunch **lays** on the kitchen table and he **proceeds** to **nibble** the **scrumptious morsels**. I **raise** one eye sleepily. I stretch, yawn and stand up.

The mouse is a **weird** earth phenomenon I have never **encountered** before? I **grab** my notebook to record my findings.

I **conduct** a thorough **investigation**, but it is too late because the little creature **scurries** to safety. I **retreat** to my **cosy** chair.

5 Cherry Gardens,
London,
WA4
Earth

Space Age Contractors,
14 Willoughby Drive.

Ref. No.: SC134567A

Dear Sir,

I am writing to express my dissatisfaction about the service I am receiving from your company, who are installing a new, state of the art, space age kitchen into my property.

When I agreed to have this work carried out, you informed me that it would take three weeks to complete. However, three months have gone by and it is still not finished. Besides this, the builders have left piles of rubbish in the front garden, which is very dangerous for my visitors. Also, there is no safe place to park their spacecraft.

Can you please make every effort to complete this work as quickly as possible, or I will refuse to pay the invoice. I will have no choice but to approach another contractor to finish the work.

Yours faithfully,

Zoggy

a wild daisy

Today, it was a beautiful day for a **walk** in the park. I **walked** through the uncut grass and **walked** slowly past the clusters of fragrant wild flowers. What joy!

Then, I **walked to** the sparkling lake, **walked** on to the muddy beach and immersed my metal toes in the cool, soothing ripples. Ducks and geese **walked** through the marshy grasses around me.

A few minutes later, I **walked** towards the overgrown path and **walked** through the roots of the straggling plants. Suddenly, I **tripped** and toppled over and lay on the ground.

A curious rat **walked** round my feet, a shy water vole **walked** past and a squirrel **ran** madly up a tree. I managed to get up and **walk** over to the bench, where a shaggy dog **walked** up to me with his tongue lolling out. This was too much! I **walked** off like a wounded solider in the direction of home.

TAKE TWO

Today, it was a beautiful day for a **stroll** in the park. I **trampled through** the uncut grass and **ambled** slowly past the clusters of fragrant wild flowers. What joy!

Then, I **approached** the sparkling lake, **continued** on to the muddy beach and immersed my metal toes in the cool, soothing ripples. Ducks and geese **waddled** through the marshy grasses around me.

A few minutes later, I **sauntered** towards the overgrown path and **clambered through** the roots of the straggling plants. Suddenly, I **stumbled** and toppled over and lay on the ground.

A curious rat **scurried** round my feet, a shy water vole **scampered** past and a squirrel **darted** madly up a tree. I managed to get up and **hobble** over to the bench, where a shaggy dog **bounded** up to me with his tongue lolling out. This was too much! I **slunk off** like a wounded solider in the direction of home.

Note the different walk words:

- *geese waddle*
- *rats scurry*
- *people stroll and amble*

SIGNS SEEN IN PARK

Danger
Deep water

OFFICIAL NOTICE   RUSHFORD COUNCIL

SWIMMING IN THE RIVER IS STRICTLY FORBIDDEN

NO CAMPING

No skateboarding

No bicycles

No ball games

ALLOWED

WARNING
STRONG CURRENT

ATTENTION
NO FLY TIPPING
24HR CCTV
IN OPERATION

| New | Reply | Reply all | Foward | Delete | Mark as | Move to |

INBOX (240)

FOLDERS

Junk (109)

Drafts (11)

Sent

Deleted (15)

New Folder

Complaint: Severely Overgrown Path

Rushford Council
To info@rushford.gov.uk

21/05/2018
Reply

Dear Sir or Madam,

I am writing to complain about the overgrown path around the lake. It is a hazard. On a recent walk, I tripped and fell, bruising my leg.

We are continually advised to exercise daily, but the path is so over grown, with stinging nettles and straggly shrubs, that it is becoming too dangerous to venture along this route. Besides this, it is over run with vermin: rats, mice and squirrels. The lake is also heavily polluted and covered in algae.

It is essential that the council clean up this area and clear the rubbish that is strewn all along the path. We want this area returned to its former beauty.

Many thanks in advance,

Yours faithfully,

Zoggy

5 Cherry Gardens,
London,
WA4
Earth

Healthy Days Magazine,
Clear Water Industrial Estate
Raines,
GH12 6DF.

Dear Dr Sharma,

I wish to respond to your article which appeared in 'Healthy Days' magazine on 25th July. I was very interested to hear about the help and support you give to people with hay fever.

Having recently moved into the area, I have developed some serious health issues. I cannot go out into the fresh air without constantly coughing, sneezing and my eyes watering. I believe I am suffering from hay fever.

I would really appreciate it if you could send me a copy of your booklet, 'How To Treat Hay Fever', to the address at the top of this letter.

Yours Sincerely,

Zoggy

MEETING MY NEIGHBOURS

 Transcript of conversation...

"An alien, did you say an alien?" **said** Dan.

"Yes! He's moved in to number 7," **said** Jack.

"Hope he won't create a disturbance," **said** Dan.

"This has always been a quiet road."

"That's right," **said** Jack.

"Perhaps we should pop in and introduce ourselves," **said** Jack.

"Good idea," **said** Dan.

The neighbours knock on the door.

"Coming," **said** Zoggy. "I'm coming. Just got to finish my live report on 'Sky Time' to Zen."

"Sounds a bit ..." **said** Dan quietly to his friend.

"Touchy..." **said** Jack.

"Greetings from Zen," **said** Zoggy, throwing the door wide open and shaking their hands firmly, as he has seen earth people do.

"Good to meet you," **said** Dan nervously.

"Do step inside," **said** Zoggy. "Excuse the chaos. I've not finished sorting things out," he said.

"Are you sure you don't mind?" **said** Dan, walking in.

"Amazing place! You have a lot of technology," **said** Jack.

"I need it to communicate with my family in Zen."

"I hear you come from outer space."

"Yes a universe 10 million light years from here."

"How long does it take you to get back?" **said** Dan.

"No more than an hour," **said** Zoggy, "with my top of the range zennel space craft."

"Wow! Awesome!" **said** Dan and Jack in amazement.

"By the way," **said** Jack, "just a word of warning, the residents committee doesn't like space craft parked in the street."

"I'll try and keep it in the garage," **said** Zoggy.

"Noisy parties don't go down well either," **said** Jack.

"When I have visitors, I'll put on silent mode," **said** Zoggy smiling.

The neighbours exchanged glances.

Human boy and girl

TAKE TWO

"An alien, did you say an alien?" **asked** Dan.

"Yes! He's moved into number 7," **replied** Jack.

"Hope he won't create a disturbance," **added** Dan. "This has always been a quiet road."

"That's right," **grunted** Jack. "Perhaps we should pop in and introduce ourselves," **suggested** Jack.

"Good idea," **agreed** Dan.

The neighbours knock on the door.

"Coming," **shrieked** Zoggy. "I'm coming. Just going to finish my live report on 'Sky Time' to Zen."

"Sounds a bit ..." **confided** Dan quietly to his friend.

"Touchy..." **continued** Jack.

"Greetings from Zen," **exclaimed** Zoggy, throwing the door wide open and shaking their hands firmly.

"Good to meet you," **uttered** Dan nervously.

"Do step inside," **muttered** Zoggy, "excuse the chaos. I've not finished sorting things out," he **whispered**.

"Are you sure you don't mind?" **responded** Dan, walking in.

"Amazing place! You have a lot of technology, **gasped** Jack.

"I need it to communicate with my family in Zen," the alien **remarked**.

"I hear you come from outer space," he **probed** gently.

"Yes a universe 10 million light years from here," he **answered**.

"How long does it take you to get back?" **inquired** Dan.

"No more than an hour," **stated** Zoggy, with my top of the range zennel space craft."

"Wow! Awesome!" **expressed** Dan and Jack in amazement.

"By the way," **informed** Jack, "just a word of warning, the residents committee doesn't like space craft parked in the street."

"I'll try and keep it in the garage," **reassured** Zoggy.

"Noisy parties don't go down well either," **revealed** Jack.

"When I have visitors, I'll put on silent mode," **declared** Zoggy smiling.

The neighbours exchange glances.

Zoggy's new neighbours invite him to a party. Shall he go or not?
Which letter do you think he should write?

Dear neighbours,

Many thanks for your kind invitation. I regret that/ I am writing to apologise that I am unable to attend your party on the 23rd June. I will be thinking of you on this special day and hope that you have a great time.

Best Wishes,

Zoggy

Dear neighbours,

Many thanks for your kind invitation. I will be delighted to attend. I look forward to seeing you on the day.

Best Wishes,

Zoggy

MY VISIT TO A POPULAR EARTH RESTAURANT

YUM!

What did I _eat_ for my first earth meal?

For the starter I _eat_ ....

For the main course I _eat_ ....

For the dessert I _eat_ ....

Write these sentences replacing the word 'eat' with a better word like:

choose   select

ask for   demand

order   opt for

Umm... perhaps my selection is a little unhealthy?

The diners in the restaurant kept giving me shifty looks. Why? What did I do wrong?

WHAT HAPPENED...

Entering the restaurant, I ask for a table; the waiter shows me to my place and I sit down. I **look at** the menu and order some **nice** human food.

I **eat** my starter cautiously, which consists of lobster and crab garnished with salad leaves.

Next, I **eat** my main course, which comprises of a lamb chop and steamed vegetables.

After this, I **eat** my dessert greedily, like a hungry wolf - consisting of fresh pineapple slices and Cornish ice cream.

I **eat** heartily... but you can not expect me to eat like a human. I prefer to **eat** my food in one gulp.

Next, I **lean** back in my chair, sigh and rub my tummy because I am **feeling rather full**.

Mimicking the other diners, I **wave over** the waiter to **ask** for the bill. Immediately, the waiter **comes over** with the chip and pin machine.

Oh no! I have no bank card. Will I be made to do the washing up?

The waiter **eyes** the carpet in **horror** because **most of** the food is on the floor.

Apparently, table manners are very important to humans...

TAKE TWO

Read, cover and write your own version.

Entering the restaurant, I ask for a table; the waiter shows me to my place and I sit down. I **browse** the menu and order some **mouth watering** human food.

I **nibble** my starter cautiously, which consists of lobster and crab garnished with salad leaves.

Next, I **munch on** my main course, which comprises of a lamb chop and steamed vegetables.

After this, I **devour** my dessert greedily, like a hungry wolf - composed of fresh pineapple slices and Cornish ice cream

I **consume** my food heartily... but you can not expect met to **chew** up my food like a human. I prefer to **swallow** it in one gulp.

I **recline** back in my chair, sigh and rub my tummy because I have **overindulged**.

Mimicking the other diners, I **summon** the waiter to **demand** the bill. Immediately, the waiter **approaches** with the chip and pin machine.

Oh no! I have no bank card. Will I be made to do the washing up?

The waiter **observes** the carpet in **dismay** because **the majority** of the food is on the floor.

Be careful Zoggy you will get *overweight*, **obese**, plump, **tubby**, podgy, plump, *rounded* and **fat** if you overindulge that much!

What did I think of the menu?

YUM!

AMAZING	DELICIOUS	YUMMY
DELECTABLE	SCRUMPTIOUS	APPETIZING
TASTY	MOUTH WATERING	DELIGHTFUL

YUK!

GHASTLY	DISGUSTING	REVOLTING
BAD	HORRIBLE	REPULSIVE
SICKENING	AWFUL	DREADFUL
HORRID	UNSPEAKABLE	ATROCIOUS

Write a review to show what I thought, in a few paragraphs.

....
....
....
....
....
....
....
....
....

5 Cherry Gardens,
London,
WA4

Taste of Britain Restaurant,
Rushford,
RF15 5PA.

Dear Sir or Madam,

Please accept my sincere apologies for leaving the restaurant hastily on Friday, without paying the bill. It was my first trip to an Earth restaurant. In my rush, to arrive promptly at 7.30 p.m., I completely forgot to inform the Bank of Zen that I wished to use my debit card on an alien planet, so I had no cash.

I would like to say that the menu was absolutely superb in your restaurant. I would definitely recommend the food to my friends. In particular, I thought the braised lamb chop with steamed vegetables was absolutely delicious.

I enclose the money I owe you to pay for the meal, which amounts to £... I would like to thank you for being so understanding and not forcing me to do the washing up.

I look forward to seeing you again soon,

Yours Faithfully,

Zoggy

DRIVING MY NEW CAR ON EARTH

Rewrite the passage choosing the best words. Why not look in the dictionary for more choices?

I ~~want~~ .... *(desire, crave, yearn for)* my own little car, so I ~~draw~~ .... *(sketch, design, draft)* one on my tablet (the latest Zen computer).

Using my exceptional alien powers, I download a car, get in and embark on a journey.

Soon I am taking a ~~drive~~ .... *(a spin, a trip, a journey, an excursion, a run)* down the motorway.

Though I haven't ~~driven~~ .... *(operated, handled, steered, manoeuvred, controlled)* a car before, I ~~try~~ .... *(attempt, endeavour, undertake, strive, aim)* to drive safely.

I ~~drive~~ .... *(steer, travel)*, along the road at a very fast speed, ~~taking no notice of~~ .... *(oblivious to, ignoring, disregarding, discounting, overlooking, paying no attention to)* speed restrictions.

TAKE CARE! BE VIGILANT. STAY ALERT. PAY ATTENTION ZOGGY!

UMMM... maybe I was going too fast...

What is that blue flashing light? Oh no! The traffic police are ~~approaching~~ .... *(advancing, catching up, coming near)*.

I do not ~~have~~ .... *(possess, hold)* a driving license. I don't have my car taxed or insured. Will I get away with a caution for my first offence? Will I go to earth prison?

I do not want to experience an earth prison, so I ~~use~~ .... *(practise, apply, utilize)* my special alien powers to make myself invisible.

The police are ~~confused~~ .... *(puzzled, perplexed, baffled, mystified, bewildered)* that an empty car is parked on the motorway. They make arrangements to have it towed away.

I ~~start~~ .... *(commence, set off, begin)* to walk home to the safety of my spacecraft.

Rewrite the story and make it more interesting. Choose from the words in the brackets, or use a thesaurus to find your own vocabulary.

RUSHFORD POLICE DEPARTMENT
POLICE REPORT

Case No: 6008923

Date: October 12th

Reporting Officer: Dan Stevens

Witness: Morwenna Frankson

Incident: Speeding on Motorway

On Wednesday 12th October, we were driving along the motorway when we saw a ferrari hurtling towards us at a phenomenal speed. The driver must have been travelling around 90 mph - the wrong way up the motorway. We radioed for assistance; the driver was out of control.

Within seconds, another police car arrived and gave chase, causing the driver to swerve onto the hard shoulder and come to a sharp halt. However, when the police officer went round to the front seat, there was no sign of a driver or any passenger in the car. The police helicopter circled the surrounding area, but could not find any trace of the offending motorist.

According to witness statements, the driver was wearing what appeared to be a metallic fancy dress costume. We are still making enquiries and appealing for more witnesses to come forward. The driver has committed a serious offence. We believe the car was stolen and had no tax or insurance. It is also possible the driver does not possess a valid UK driving licence.

CAN YOU **SEE** ME?

PERCEIVE   LOOK   NOTICE   OBSERVE

SIGHT   GLIMPSE   SPOT   DETECT

WHERE AM I?

Today I decided to challenge the Earthlings...

The question I asked: "How many better words for 'see' can you think of?"

MY SCHOOL DAY

*What can I **learn** at an earth school that will be useful to planet Zen?*

My Observations...

In science, I **learn** some important scientific facts about earth. In maths, I **learn** some essential formulas. In English, I **see** some people need a bit of Zoggy help with spelling, grammar and punctuation, but I **see** there are some great novels to be read in English literature.

Then, in the afternoon, I **see** that painting in art is very relaxing, I **see** that P.E. will improve my physical fitness while, in geography, I **see** that I will be able to collect some useful information about Earth.

In history, I do not **see** how I will ever remember all those facts.

Worse than this, I **see** that I.T. is much too easy. The computer systems are so out of date.

*I AM **SHOCKED**... Earthlings have much to learn from Zen!*

TAKE TWO

*I **fathom** that Earth people consider learning to be important and so I **understand** why children go to school.*

In science, I **discover** some important scientific facts about earth. In maths I **grasp** some essential formulas. In English, I **conclude** that there are some earth people who need a bit of Zoggy help with spelling, grammar and punctuation, but I **acknowledge** that there are some great novels to be read in English literature.

Then, in the afternoon, I **appreciate** that painting in art is very relaxing, I **admit** that P.E. will improve my physical fitness while, in geography, I **determine** that I will be able to collect some useful information about earth.

In history, I fail to **comprehend** how I will ever remember all those facts.

Worse than this, I **perceive** that I.T. is much too easy. I am shocked by the out of date computer systems.

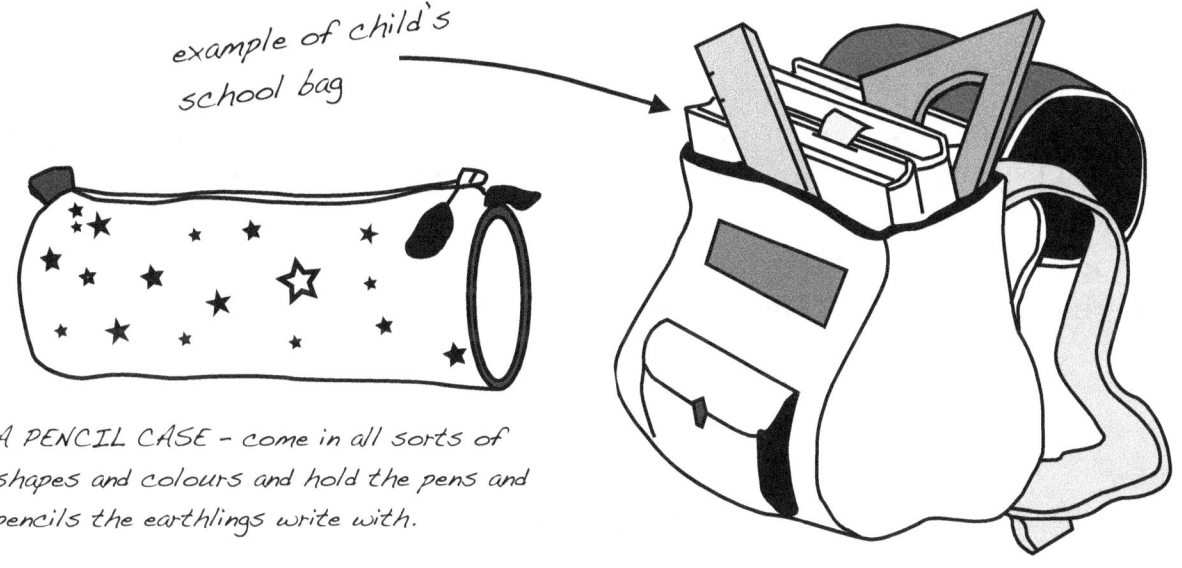

example of child's school bag

A PENCIL CASE - come in all sorts of shapes and colours and hold the pens and pencils the earthlings write with.

Some of the children are carrying letters written by their parents. Zoggy is very curious. He takes a peep.

Dear Miss Taylor,

My daughter has been unable to hand in her homework, because she dropped it in the snow. She will rewrite it and hand it in tomorrow. Thank you for your understanding.

                              Yours Sincerely,

                              Caroline Duckett

Dear Mr Bruce,

My son was unable to attend school yesterday, because he was suffering from a stomach upset. He feels much better today.

Please advise me of any work he has missed, so we can catch up at home.

                              Yours Sincerely,

                              Sarah Lucas

Dear Mrs Hathaway,

I would like to inform you that my son will be leaving at the end of the term. I have taken a new job in Cardiff, so he will be transferring to the Cardiff Boys School.

I would like to take this opportunity to thank you for all the encouragement you have given him over the last two years.

                              Yours Sincerely,

                              Brian Freedman

EXPLORING EARTH

The people of Earth thoroughly enjoy all of these activities....

What can an alien do on earth?

First, I **go** to the leisure complex. I **go up** the escalator to the shopping mall and then **go down**. I **go up and down** several times. This is cool.

When I get bored, I **go** into a fashion store, but sadly there are no designer outfits that fit an alien.

After this, I **go** to the 3D multi screen cinema, but the glasses do not fit my alien eyes. Rubbish!

I **go** on a trip to the kids play zone. I **go** up the rock face, I **go** on the trampoline and **go** round the roller-skating course.

Next, I **go** outside to survey the assault course. I swing on the tyre, although my arms and legs are not made for human activities. My body is too metallic. How frustrating!

Finally, I **go back** to the library and sit at a computer.

I am most definitely back in my comfort zone.

TAKE TWO

Umm... the leisure complex sounds so, so, so boring with so many words like 'go'. Rewrite the passage and replace the underlined words with more interesting vocabulary.

First, I **visit** the leisure complex. I **ascend** the escalator to the shopping mall and then **descend**. I **ascend and descend** several times. This is amazing.

When I get bored, I **enter** a fashion store, but there are no designer outfits that suit an alien.

After this, I **proceed** to the 3D multi screen cinema, but the glasses do not fit my alien eyes. Rubbish!

I **embark** on a trip to the kids play zone. First, I **attempt** to climb the rock face, I **endeavour** to keep my balance on the trampoline and **tackles a** roller-skating course.

Next, I **venture** outside to survey the assault course. I swing on the tyre, but my alien arms and legs are not cut out for human activities. My body is too metallic. How frustrating!

Finally, I **retreat** to the library and sit at a computer. I am definitely back in my comfort zone.

Human child climbing rock face... I feel very embarrassed at my feeble attempt - i am not at all flexible.

| New | Reply | Reply all | Foward | Delete | Mark as | Move to |

INBOX (240)

FOLDERS

Junk (109)

Drafts (11)

Sent

Deleted (15)

New Folder

Customer Complaint

Sports Shop 21/05/2018
To storemanager@sportsshop.com   Reply

Dear Sir or Madam,

I recently bought some trainers from your store. They are top of the range, designer trainers and cost over £100. Unfortunately, the first time I wore them they fell apart.

The quality of these trainers is appalling and they are not worth the money I paid for them. For this price, I would expect them to last longer than one wear.

Unfortunately, I have lost the receipt, but I believe I am entitled to a full refund, as they were not fit for purpose. If this is not possible, I will accept a credit voucher, so I can purchase a new pair.

I look forward to hearing from you,

Zoggy

Use the list of words on page 63 to replace the words in bold.

MY BIG NIGHT OUT

First, I see a **grand** building with a neon sign flashing on and off above the door - 'The Royal Theatre.' There is a show on tonight starting at 7.30pm. It is **a popular** musical starring some **well-known** celebrities.

I am eagerly **anticipating** the show.

I tag on the end of the queue of earth people, but I am not sufficiently **tall** to reach up to the window of the ticket kiosk (which is just as well as I don't possess earth money).

Now I **clamber up** the stairs, swept along in the **immense crowd** of theatre goers, dodging the officials on the door that are checking tickets.

Soon, I **gain access** to a huge darkened hall, filled with rows of plush red velvet chairs and perch on the front row of the circle, **surveying** the scene around me. **A huge** red curtain conceals the stage; musicians play harmoniously on strange instruments.

I **lean** over the balcony precariously, to the horror of the elderly lady in the next seat. It is a big drop and I start to feel a bit dizzy. I **scan** my programme, **savouring** my popcorn (which I found laying on the stairs as I made my way up).

The auditorium is **packed**, the theatre-goers chat together **exuberantly** and I feel a buzz of excitement.

After a few minutes, an announcement is made to **turn off** all mobile phones, so I check my computer is on 'sleep mode' and **recline** back in my chair, not knowing what to expect.

To my delight, the curtain **goes up** and the entertainment **begins**. The actors and actresses **perform** on the stage, **wearing** flamboyant costumes in bright colours. They start to sing and dance.

I like the rhythm. I **rock to** the beat, and I feel like joining in. I feel an urge to tap my metal toes and jig my metal body around, so I **move** into the aisle to dance.

"Please sit down. You are creating a **disturbance**," demands the elderly lady.
"Yes, please sit down," **complain** other members of the audience angrily.

In an instant, a hand **comes down** on my metal body and marches me back to my seat with a warning.
"Sit down, or you will be escorted out," **reprimands** the usher sternly.

I fidget in my seat. I find it **difficult** to sit still because I don't understand the story and I am **aware** that the lady next to me is scowling in my direction.

Fortunately, the interval comes quickly. I **glance** around. Why are people **getting up** in the middle of the performance? I join another queue. It is long and I wonder whether I will still be queuing when the performance starts again. I **push myself** to the front of the queue.

I reach out to take a share of the food but the usherette states sternly,
"No money, no ice cream."
"Please...?" I whimper, looking pleadingly at her. The tub of ice cream is thrust at me.
"Take it, but don't breath a word to anyone, or I will lose my position." I **take it enthusiastically** and **swallows** it in one gulp.

My seat in the theatre...

Now the music starts again. I **go back** to my seat. Everyone reluctantly stands up, so I can reach my chair which is right in the middle of a row. I **squeeze** past.

When the show starts again, the music is even louder and vibrates in my metal ears, having a hypnotising effect on me. I **hear** the beat of the drums, the **sound** of guitars and I have to stand up. I have to **wave** my antennae; I have to jig up and down - I am rocking.

The woman beside me is furious, whilst people behind are **bellowing**, "Sit down. You're spoiling the show for others."

Next, I feel the same hand come down on my metal frame. I am being **lifted up** and up, high into the air and am thrust towards the exit, along a narrow corridor and through two heavy doors - my metal frame **discarded** in a heap on the pavement outside. Crash!

The theatre door slams shut. Crowds of pedestrians push past, pretending not to see a lost alien in trouble. I recompose myself, stand up and continue on my way.

Read, cover and write your own version. Look up any words you don't understand in the dictionary.

HELPFUL WORDS

Replace the underlined words in the previous story with the appropriate word or phrase from the list below. Remember, it is important to use the right word in the right place.

chucked	commences	consumes	bends	dance to
clamour	eagerly	in high spirits	rebukes	an extensive
famous	an impressive	accepts it	conscious	crammed
scrambles up	raised up	proceeds to	disruption	screaming
returns	admonish	proceeds	lofty	scrutinizing
an acclaimed	gazes at	clothed in	challenging	gains entry
moving	descends	relishing	gesticulate	listens to
thrusts himself forward	multitude	look	switch off	lounges
forces his way	rises	awaiting	massive	warns

ANSWERS *How did you do?*

grand	an impressive	moves	proceeds
a popular	an acclaimed	disturbance	disruption
well-known	famous	complain	admonish
anticipating	awaiting	comes down	descends
tall	lofty	reprimands	rebukes
clambers up	scrambles up	difficult	challenging
immense crowd	multitude	aware	conscious
gains access	gains entry	glance	look
surveying	scrutinizing	getting up	moving
a huge	an extensive	pushes himself	thrusts himself forward
leans	bends	takes it	accepts it
scans	gazes at	enthusiastically	eagerly
savouring	relishing	swallows	consumes
packed	crammed	goes back	returns
exuberantly	in high spirits	squeezes	forces his way
turn off	switch off	hears	listens to
reclines	lounges	sound	clamour
ascends	rises	wave	gesticulate
begins	commences	bellowing	screaming
perform	act	lifted up	raised up
wearing	clothed in	discarded	chucked
rock to	dance to		

THE DAILY STAR

ARTS & ENTERTAINMENT

THEATRE

A Spectacular Success

Rock A Bye Baby
London Palladian, Oct 12th
Until January 31st
Reviewed by Damien Blake

London's Palladian Theatre saw the opening night of a new musical called 'Rock A Bye Baby' starring Tanya O'Brien, Jason Mumford and Frances Fields.

The show was a spectacular success. The cast of eight played their parts brilliantly and the audience was entranced. The stage effects were outstanding.

"This was an extremely colourful rendering of the story," stated John Marsh, a theatrical critic. "It is one of the most quality shows of all times" added The Stage Magazine. The

lively beat of the music really makes the audience get on their feet and join in.

The opening night was a great success, except for a small disturbance from a member of the audience, who had to be removed from the auditorium.

MY BIG MISTAKE

Use the helpful words to fill in the blanks.

I try to get fit but it all goes wrong...

I .... a place with an inviting sign.

'Welcome. Join our gym. Memberships slashed to half price, this week only.'

I .... a crowd of people in a queue. Because I am so short, I have no trouble .... the reception desk (which is .... for me because I have no earth cheque book or bank card).

I .... the signs, past the changing rooms, into a room full of .... machines and I .... a buzz of excitement. Earthlings are exercising to loud rock music. I observe that humans do not choose to walk in the fresh air, but .... to walk on walking machines!

I .... the running machine and jog up and down until I am gasping for breath; I sit .... the rowing machine and pull with all my might; pedal .... on the cycling machine and lift the weights until I am ....

Next, I decide to .... the swimming pool. I've never swum before, but it looks quite easy. On arriving at the poolside, I stick one of my metal toes into the water to .... the temperature of the pool. It's warm — lovely and warm so I .... my whole body in, but I am out of my depth and I am going down, down, down under the deep water! I gasp, gurgle and ...., as I try to breathe under the water and I thrash about .... I have water in my eyes, my nose and my mouth! It is penetrating my metal interior and shorting out my electric circuits.

The lifeguard ………………… my cry for help and ………………… in quickly to rescue me. He grabs me, hauls me out of the water and attempts to resuscitate me, but there is ……………………… of life (because I have automatically shut down my computer network.) The lifeguard calls 999 for an ambulance.

Before I know it, I am ……………………………… to hospital in an ambulance. I am taken ………………… to the accident and emergency department - the cardio resuscitation unit. The doctor ………………………… up to the heart monitor. It has a very strange reading.

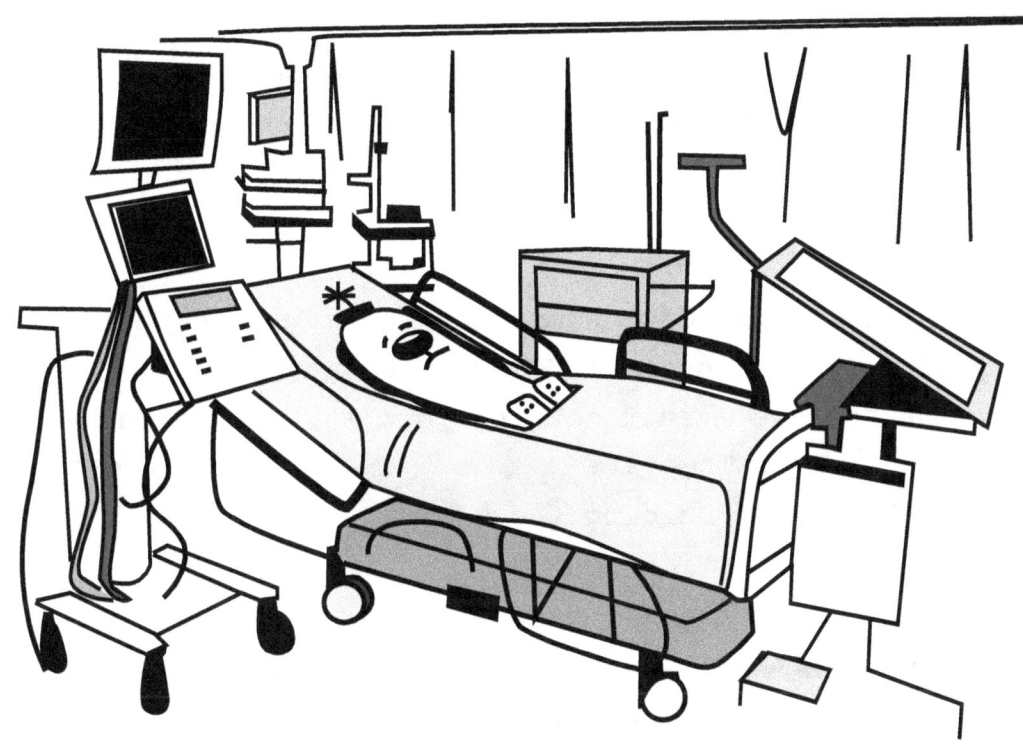

They ………………… my breathing, my pulse, my blood pressure and take an x ray. The readings cause ……………… because they are ………………… Meanwhile I am stirring, my computer is automatically turning on to waking mode. The doctors are …………………………; the patient is not responding like a normal human being. I have no pulse, because I have no blood. The high tech equipment ………………………… The doctors ………………………… a medical emergency.

The patient is a creature that has not been previously …………………………; a creature that has never been seen before.

69

What shall we do? Who do we call? Do we call MI5? Do we send him to the Unit for Tropical Diseases? Do we alert the army? Do we phone for the police?

They radio out **RED ALERT.**

Stand by! **THERE'S AN *ALIEN* INVASION!**

I am coming round. My computer system is fully working and I am becoming conscious. What's that strong smell of disinfectant I think to myself? Where am I? I am being wheeled on a trolley to a secure room and the door is being firmly ……………………………

I ……………………!

There is no time to be lost. Summoning all my strength together and every bit of brainpower, I focus on my spacecraft. I picture it in my mind and see myself getting into it. What's that? Some men are …………………… They are …………………… round the door, peering in, their eyes bulging.

ZOOM! In an agonising moment, my special alien powers …………………… me out of the hospital - back, back, back to my holiday home, where I …………………… …………………… the rest of my possessions, especially the notebook, where I have written my observations of earth, used on my spying missions. In a second, I have finished packing and load everything into my spacecraft.

Then **ZOOOOOOOOOM UP, UP, UP!**

ZOOOOOOOOOOM UP, UP, UP!

GOOD BYE
EARTH.

SEE YOU SOON.

Read on...

The men in the military uniforms, followed by the police, doctors, personnel from MI5 and four government officials, throw open the door in anticipation..... but IV'E GONE!

They .... the room, but there is no sign of me.

I have vanished into thin air.

"........................", comments one of the doctors. "If I had not seen it with my own eyes, I would never have .... it."

The men in military uniform, the police, MI5 and government officials look .... at the doctors.

"We have the X ray pictures," insist the third doctor, ... the photographs into the hands of the official men.

"Very strange indeed," they remark incredulously.

GRAMMAR CHECK

A quick look at the basics of English grammar.

Of course, there is loads more to learn, but this is all we have room for here in this book.

A formal letter is set out like this:

> My address,
> Town,
> Post code
>
> Date.
>
> The name of the person,
> The business address,
> Town.
>
> Dear Sir or Madame,
>
> I am writing to enquire about ....
> ....
> ....
> ....
> ....
> ....
> ....
>
> Yours faithfully,
>
> Zoggy

	use	
For Mr/ Mrs/ Ms	→	Yours Sincerely
For Dear Friend	→	Best Wishes / Love From
For Sir/ Madam	→	Yours Faithfully

To write well you must aim your writing at the right people.

Writing can be:

FORMAL

Formal writing uses standard English. This is the way a news presenter speaks. Use formal writing to people you do not know. For example, when you are writing to the council.

INFORMAL

Uses non-standard English. It uses local dialect, colloquial English or slang.

Make sure you use a variety of sentences:

SIMPLE

I am walking in Hyde Park.

COMPOUND

Compound sentences join two simple sentences using *and* or *but*.

- I am eating Cheddar cheese <u>and</u> I don't like it.

- I tripped walking round The Serpentine <u>but</u> did not fall.

COMPLEX

Use a phrase or conjunction to join ideas in complex sentences.

- As I am in London, I'm visiting the famous Westminster Abbey.

- I love the Sunset over the Thames because the sky is a red ball of fire.

- I am shopping in Oxford Street, until ten o'clock.

These sentences use a **subordinate clause**.

- Despite the fact I'm eating black pudding, I am enjoying my breakfast in London.

- I was walking past Buckingham Palace, when I saw soldiers marching.

This sentence has a clause in the middle of it.

- The Duck Tour, which includes a river trip, takes you all round the sights of London.

- I don't like the British weather.

   This is a **statement**.

- How tall is The Shard?

   This is a **question**.

- Mind the gap.

   This is a **command** or an **instruction**.

- That's disgusting!

   This is an **exclamation**.

In English, parts of speech include:

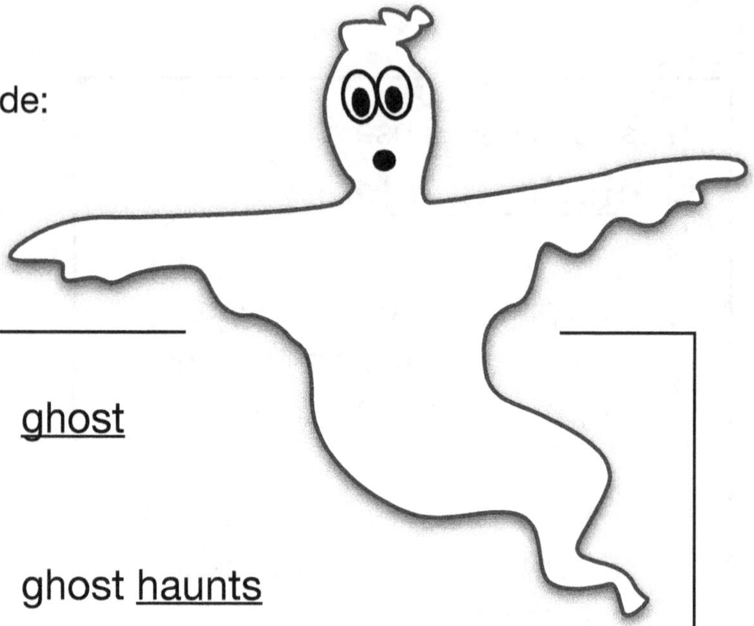

NOUN	ghost
VERB	ghost haunts
ADJECTIVES	scary ghost haunts
ADVERBS	scary ghost haunts spookily
PRONOUNS	It walks
PREPOSITIONS	up
CONJUNCTIONS	the stairs and on to the landing

The scary (*adjective*) ghost (*noun*) in (*preposition*) Hampton Court (*noun*) walks (*verb*) spookily (*adverb*) up (*preposition*) the stairs (*noun*) and (*conjunction*) across (*preposition*) the landing (*noun*).

Let's look at nouns and adjectives...

Put interesting adjectives with nouns.

ADJECTIVE	NOUN	
interesting	garden	*interesting book*
agreeable	walk	....
beautiful	book	....
fast	morning	....
delicious	dress	....
enjoyable	house	....
fine	car	....
mischievous	burger	....
pretty	toddler	....
pleasant	film	....

Remember, it is important to make your sentences more interesting by using adjectives with your nouns.

ADD A NOUN	ADD AN ADJECTIVE	
a cat	a sneaky cat	a greedy cat
a dog	a lazy dog	a fat dog
a frog	a jumpy frog	a slimy frog

Remember words have DIFFERENT MEANINGS

For each new word the most common dictionary definitions have been given.

However, when you look up the meaning of an unfamiliar word, you must decide which definition in the dictionary is the right one to fit the context of the passage you are reading

Some adjectives sound right with a particular noun. Match these adjectives to the most suitable noun.

Exercise 1

modern	suspicion
complete	expression
grim	mountain
prize	message
beautiful	technology
strong	furniture
sinister	possession
distant	surprise
valuable	scenery
antique	treasure

Exercise 2

savage	cardboard
stern	joke
bloodthirsty	teacher
serious	performance
hilarious	measures
luscious	evidence
incompetent	monster
outstanding	warrior
flimsy	fruit
insufficient	consideration

ANSWERS *Did you get them right?*

EXERCISE 1

modern	technology
complete	surprise
grim	expression
prize	possession
beautiful	scenery
strong	suspicion
sinister	message
distant	mountain
valuable	treasure
antique	furniture

EXERCISE 2

savage	warrior
stern	measures
bloodthirsty	monster
serious	consideration
hilarious	joke
luscious	fruit
incompetent	teacher
outstanding	performance
flimsy	cardboard
insufficient	evidence

Match the adjectives to the most suitable noun.

EXERCISE 3

torrential	teenager
shrewd	mind
elderly	expression
sprightly	old man
chaotic	neighbourhood
inquiring	rain
lavish	mess
sulky	person
affluent	politician
solemn	lifestyle

EXERCISE 4

aggressive	identity
candid	warning
impressive	coincidence
official	home
cultural	dressing
amazing	indignation
righteous	behaviour
sterile	words
harsh	opinion

ANSWERS *Did you get them right?*

EXERCISE 3

torrential	rain
shrewd	politician
elderly	person
sprightly	old man
chaotic	mess
inquiring	mind
lavish	lifestyle
sulky	teenager
affluent	neighbourhood
solemn	expression

EXERCISE 4

aggressive	behaviour
candid	opinion
impressive	home
official	warning
cultural	identity
amazing	coincidence
righteous	indignation
sterile	dressing
harsh	words

Some adjectives sound right with a particular noun. Match these adjectives to the most suitable noun.

Exercise 5

sumptuous	woman
generous	provision
abundant	stance
furtive	cloud
great	remark
threatening	tone
vivid	feast
brutal	achievement
acute	water
insulting	portion
slender	colour
tranquil	talent
exceptional	poverty
disdainful	glance
meagre	wage

Exercise 6

vulnerable	lifestyle
sharp	tactics
sneaky	corner
prosperous	food
secluded	pet
disdainful	child
delectable	attachment
devoted	hunt
close	smell
relentless	glance
appetising	tone
plentiful	supply
luxurious	hysteria
mass	businessman

ANSWERS *Did you get them right?*

EXERCISE 5

sumptuous	feast
generous	portion
abundant	provision
furtive	stance
great	achievement
threatening	cloud
vivid	colour
brutal	tone
acute	poverty
insulting	remark
slender	woman
tranquil	water
exceptional	talent
disdainful	glance
meagre	wage

EXERCISE 6

vulnerable	child
sharp	tone
sneaky	tactics
prosperous	businessman
secluded	corner
disdainful	glance
delectable	food
devoted	pet
close	attachment
relentless	hunt
appetising	smell
plentiful	supply
luxurious	lifestyle
mass	hysteria

Let's look at verbs...

An **ACTIVE VERB** is underlined in the sentence below.

The girl ate the chocolate bar.

The subject of this sentence is 'the girl' so she does the action.

A **PASSIVE VERB** is underlined in the sentence below.

The chocolate bar was eaten by the girl.

In this sentence, the chocolate bar is the subject and has the action done to it.

Write the following sentences using passive verbs.

Sam broke the vase.
The vase was broken by Sam.

1. The decorator painted the wall.

   ....

2. The cat pounced on the mouse.

   The mouse was ....

3. The racing drivers drove the car.

   The car was ....

4. The robber burgled the house.

   The house was ....

5. The heavy rain caused a flood.

   The flood was ....

REPLACE that bossy word '<u>GET</u>.'

GET TO	GET BACK	GET UP
arrive	recover	arise
come	repossess	rise
reach	regain	stand
land at	recuperate	wake up
touch down at	reclaim	awaken
GET BY	**GET ROUND**	**GET HOLD OF**
exist	persuade	achieve
manage	win over	attain
get along	convince	obtain
cope	sway	acquire
GET OUT	**GET IT**	find
escape	fathom	search out
evade	understand	dig up
dodge	latch on	come into
retreat	comprehend	possession of
evacuate	grasp	fetch
break out	see	hunt
		secure
GET OVER	**GET OFF/DOWN**	**GET TOGETHER**
survive	alight	congregate
live through	descend	gather
recover from	dismount	meet
		assemble
		gather

Read through the words on the previous page. Cover and write.
How many can you remember?

GET TO	GET BACK	GET UP
....	....	....
....	....	....
....	....	....
....	....	....
....	....	....

GET BY	GET ROUND	GET HOLD OF
....	....	....
....	....	....
....	....	....
....	....	....
		....

GET OUT	GET IT	
....	....	....
....	....	....
....	....	....
....	....	....
....	....	....
....	....	....

GET OVER	GET OFF/DOWN	GET TOGETHER
....	....	....
....	....	....
....	....	....
		....
		....

I have decided to teach the people of Earth some <u>even harder verbs</u>.

```
discuss        evade         comprehend

confide        strive        imagine

amend          respect       dispense

reveal         impart
```

SHALL I <u>EXTERMINATE</u> THESE WORDS?   NO!

WHAT THEY MEAN...

Let's match each harder verb to a group of words with a similar meaning. Can you add other words?

---

fathom
perceive
understand
grasp

is the same as

com..........

---

alter
change
improve
modify

is the same as

am..........

---

communicate
make known
confide
disclose

is the same as

im..........

---

conceive
devise
envisage
conjure up

means

ima..........

---

deal out
allocate
allot
distribute

means

dis..........

---

debate
deliberate
consult with
exchange views

means

disc..........

---

avoid
escape
get away from
dodge

means

ev..........

---

admit to
divulge
confess
disclose

means

con..........

---

attempt
endeavour to
exert oneself
to do all one can

means

str..........

---

give away   make known   show   uncover   esteem   honour   value

means   means

rev..........   res..........

Let's look at verbs and adverbs...

Underline the verbs and adverbs in these sentences.

> The baby **chuckled** (verb) **happily** (adverb).
>
> 1. The dog snored loudly on the rug.
> 2. In the test, the students scribbled hurriedly.
> 3. The eagle swooped aggressively at its prey.
> 4. The politician argued skilfully.
> 5. The audience waited expectantly for the film to start.
> 6. Richard read his book eagerly.
> 7. The athlete raced energetically past the finish line.
> 8. Dad shouted angrily at Kim.
> 9. A fox crept cunningly into the garden.
> 10. The boat swayed violently on the waves.

Find a noun, adjective, verb and adverb in these sentences. Write them in the chart below.

> 1. The ferocious dog barked loudly at the people who opened the gate.
> 2. The little brown mouse crept softly through the grass.
> 3. The huge stripy tiger prowled proudly through the jungle.
> 4. The cute rabbit ran playfully round the room.
> 5. The ginger cat watched the mouse hole attentively everyday.

ADJECTIVE	NOUN	VERB	ADVERB
ferocious	dog	barked	loudly
....	....	....	....
....	....	....	....
....	....	....	....
....	....	....	....

Write some more simply, super sentences with nouns, verbs, adjectives and adverbs.

Zoggy says, "Fill in the page to check your grammar.
Match the verb with the most suitable adverb. There is more than one choice.

VERB	ADVERB
walk	ravenously
argue	happily
arrive	bravely
stroll	energetically
eat	politely
growl	respectfully
watch	aimlessly
knock	ferociously
wait	loudly
act	recklessly
sneak	badly
follow	deeply
care	closely
love	patiently
shout	furtively
volunteer	flatly
fight	faithfully
behave	tirelessly
answer	tenderly
interrupt	suspiciously
live	quickly
jump	aggressively
refuse	promptly
treat	dangerously
gobble	rudely
drive	loudly
work	greedily

Use the right pronoun

We do not need to repeat nouns or naming words because we can use pronouns. They take the place of peoples' names and become the subject.

FIRST PERSON	SECOND PERSON	THIRD PERSON
I	you	he/she
we	your	it
my		they

SINGULAR PRONOUNS - I, she, he, it

PLURAL PRONOUNS - we, they

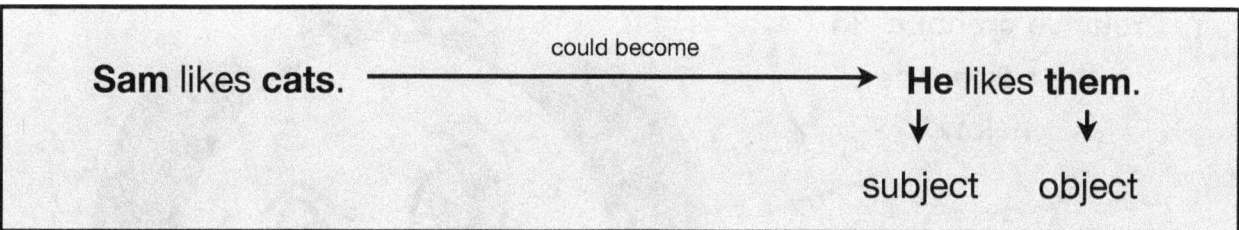

Some examples of pronouns...

    PERSONAL: I, we, he, she, it, they, me, you

    POSSESSIVE: ours, mine, yours, hers, his, its, theirs

    RELATIVE: what, which, that, who, whom, whose

    DEMONSTRATIVE: this, that, these, those

Replace the words in brackets with pronouns.

> (Ben) .... walked into the classroom with (his mum) ....
>
> They looked at (the pictures on the wall) ....,
>
> "Which one is (your picture) ....?"
>
> "That one is (my picture) ...."

'Who' and 'which' are _relative pronouns_.

- Use 'who' when writing about people.

    The girl, who fell over at school, was taken to hospital.

- Use 'which' when writing about things or animals.

    The stray kitten, which arrived at our door, did not have an owner.

"Spot the relative pronouns in the sentences below."

1. The new book, which was on sale at midnight, sold hundreds of copies.

2. The boy found a necklace, which he took to the police.

3. The man, who rescued the drowning boy, received an award.

4. The cat, which was very hungry, greedily gobbled down his dinner.

Get these right.

Wrong	Right
He is as clever as me.	He is as clever as I.
Him and me went for a walk.	He and I went for a walk.
It was her who we saw at the pool.	It was she whom we saw at the pool.
Was it him or her who won the prize?	Was it he or she who won the prize?
I met he and she in the supermarket yesterday.	I met him and her in the supermarket yesterday.

Wrong	Right
Everyone must ride their own horse.	Everyone must ride his own horse.
Neither he or she understand what they are doing.	Neither he or she understands what he or she is doing.
Everyone what wants to come on the picnic must bring their own food.	Everyone that wants to come on the picnic must bring his or her own food.

(A singular indefinite pronoun must always be singular.)

Write down some more examples.

PREPOSITIONS show a relationship to a noun.

as	in	about	below
for	from	in	into
through	off	around	like
except	during	outside	until
before	till	beneath	next
toward	concerning	despite	since

CONJUNCTIONS are joining words.

joining words	also	Persuade	Comparing	Opinions
and	plus	clearly	alternatively	one might suggest
who	because	evidently	similarly	infer
which	if	of course	nevertheless	deduce
whenever	as	obviously	on the other hand	propose
wherever	as soon as	surely	in contrast	imply
whilst	whether	certainly	however	it would seem that
whereas	**Explanatory**	**Passing of time**	but	**Stress importance**
although	hence	firstly	yet	especially
since	for example	secondly	instead	significantly
unless	furthermore	finally	despite of	above all
despite	moreover	initially	although	notably
as though	as a result of	to conclude	still	more importantly
even though	since	to sum up	equally	in particular
in spite of	consequently	subsequently	similarly	indeed
when	such as	eventually	in the same way	in fact
as well as	for instance	meanwhile	likewise	besides

Write out these sentences correcting the wrong word.

1. The apples is ripe on the tree.
2. "My toy car don't go," cried Sam.
3. The boy shouted to his friend, "You don't know nothing about football."
4. The rabbit run away when it was time to go back to its cage.
5. The proud boy congratulated hisself for winning the race.

1. Oliver brung me a present.
2. we saw squirrels in those trees.
3. I and Thomas work together.
4. "My glasses is broken," grumbled Liam.
5. Leave me to do my work.
6. I seed a ship on the horizon.
7. Give them little ones some sweets.
8. Our neighbour ask me to borrow him a bottle of milk.
9. The vet said the puppy hadn't nothing wrong with him.
10. Her elbow had wore a hole in the sleeve of her jumper.

1. There isn't nothing wrong with Marcus.
2. Sam didn't ought to go down the cliff.
3. Tom and I was waiting for the bell to ring.
4. The trainers I tried on feeled fine.
5. The strawberries is ripe. They are ready to be picked.
6. Lucy and me are good friends.

1. Mum promised she would learn me to cook.
2. The boy come to deliver the newspaper.
3. James knowed he was wrong.
4. Me and her go dancing on Tuesday.
5. The wind blewed hard last night.
6. Sue and I has to help the teacher.
7. We haven't never been to Paris.
8. Me and Louise are good friends.

---

1. Ben didn't ought to climb that tree.
2. They must speak more quieter.
3. He has ate his sweets.
4. Your friend has went on the bus alone.
5. These raspberries is sour.
6. Us girls played together.
7. The gasman come to mend the boiler.
8. Mark say to us to lend him a book.

---

1. We was given some homework on Tuesday.
2. We have bin to London to see the exhibition.
3. Emma she is nearly ten.
4. Us girls are all friends.
5. The teacher didn't tell nobody about the test.
6. Tom knowed he shouldn't pick the apples.
7. My tooths were aching.
8. My friend has went without me.

> Remember a word that means the same as another is a **synonym**.
>
> bucket → pail
>
> convenient → labour saving
>
> expect → predict → forecast
>
> impressive → dramatic
>
> bright → sharp → astute
>
> awful → deplorable

Remember **antonym** is a word that means the opposite.

swift → slow

pessimistic → optimistic

IN THE SHOP:
- jostle
- scramble
- push
- shove

IN THE CAR:
- swerve
- veer
- deviate
- turn sharply

FEEL CALM:
- cool
- dispassionate
- indifferent
- philosophical

FEEL CAUTIOUS:
- ....
- ....
- ....

FEEL SUPERIOR:
- ....
- ....
- ....

FEEL INFERIOR:
- ....
- ....
- ....

ASCEND:
- ....
- ....
- ....

DESCEND:
- ....
- ....
- ....

CHECK YOUR ANSWERS

Page 83

Beautiful garden
Pleasant walk
Interesting book
Fine morning
Pretty dress
Agreeable house
Fast car
Delicious burger
Mischievous toddler
Enjoyable film

Page 90

1. The wall was painted by the decorator
2. The mouse was pounced on by the cat
3. The car was driven by the racing driver
4. The house was burgled by the robber
5. The flood was caused by the heavy rain

Page 95

1. Snored loudly
2. Scribbled hurriedly
3. Swooped aggressively
4. Argued skilfully
5. Waited expectantly
6. Read eagerly
7. Raced energetically
8. Shouted angrily
9. Crept cunningly
10. Swayed violently

Adjective - ferocious, little brown, huge stripy, cute, ginger
Noun - dog, mouse, tiger, rabbit, cat
Verb - barked, crept, prowled, ran, watched
Adverb - loudly, softly, proudly, playfully, attentively

Page 97

He walked into the classroom with her. They looked at them.
"Which one is yours?"
"That one is mine."

Page 98

1. Which
2. Which
3. Who
4. Which

Page 101

1. The apples are ripe on the tree.
2. "My toy car doesn't go," cried Sam.
3. The boy shouted to his friend, " You don't know anything about football."
4. The rabbit ran away when it was time to go back to its cage.
5. The proud boy congratulated himself for winning the race.

1. Oliver brought me a present.
2. We saw squirrels in the trees.
3. Thomas and I work together.
4. "My glasses are broken," grumbled Liam.
5. Leave me alone to work
6. I saw a ship on the horizon.
7. Give the little ones some sweets.
8. Our neighbour asked me to lend him a bottle of milk.
9. The vet said the puppy had nothing wrong with him.
10. Her elbow had worn a hole in the sleeve of her jumper.

1. There isn't anything wrong with Marcus.
2. Sam shouldn't have gone down the cliff.
3. Tom and I were waiting for the bell to ring.
4. The trainers I tried on felt fine.
5. The strawberries are ripe. They are ready to be picked.
6. Lucy and I are good friends.

Page 102

1. Mum promised she would teach me to cook.
2. The boy came to deliver the newspaper.
3. James knew he was wrong.
4. We go dancing on Tuesday.
5. The wind blew hard last night.
6. Sue and I have to help the teacher.
7. We have never been to Paris.
8. Louise and I are good friends.

1. Ben shouldn't have climbed that tree.
2. They must speak quieter.
3. He has eaten his sweets.
4. Your friend has gone on the bus alone.
5. These raspberries are sour.
6. We played together.
7. The gasman came to mend the boiler.
8. Mark asked us to lend him a book.

1. We were given some homework on Tuesday.
2. We have been to London to se the exhibition.
3. 3. Emma is nearly ten.
4. 4. We are all friends.
5. 5. The teacher didn't tell anybody about the test.
6. 6. Tom knew he shouldn't pick the apples.
7. 7. My teeth were aching.
8. 8. My friend has gone without me.

Which **adjectives** describe Zoggy?

106

Fill in the chart:

ZOGGY WOULD LIKE TO BE:	ZOGGY WOULD NOT LIKE TO BE:
courageous	repulsive
....	....
....	....
....	....
....	....
....	....
....	....
....	....
....	....
....	....
....	....
....	....
....	....

Can you add some more words?
Check your answers in a dictionary.

In your SCHOOL REPORT...

you aim to (be):

- HIGHLY MOTIVATED
- HONEST
- COURTEOUS
- POLITE
- CARING
- HELPFUL
- FOCUSES ON TASKS
- RELIABLE
- DEPENDABLE
- RESPECTFUL
- TAKES PRIDE IN HIS/HER WORK
- RISES TO NEW CHALLENGES
- WORKS WELL INDEPENDENTLY
- ADAPTS EASILY TO NEW SITUATIONS
- HARDWORKING
- CONSCIENTIOUS
- ENTHUSIASTIC LEARNER
- POSITIVE INFLUENCE
- MAKES GOOD PROGRESS
- PUTS IN A LOT OF EFFORT
- ACTIVELY PARTICIPATES IN DISCUSSION
- GOOD REASONING ABILITY

Applying to college, university or for a job...

I am <u>versatile</u>, <u>flexible</u> and very <u>adaptable</u>.

I have excellent <u>verbal and written communication skills</u>.

I am <u>able to relate to a wide variety of people</u>.

I am <u>confident working under pressure</u> and <u>multi-tasking</u>.

I am...

<u>self-motivated</u>

<u>self-disciplined</u>

<u>dedicated</u>

<u>organised</u>

I am extremely <u>creative</u> and skilled at <u>solving problems</u>.

I am a highly <u>analytical</u> and <u>logical thinker</u>.

I am <u>willing to learn</u> and <u>eager to meet new challenges</u>.

"Phew..."

> When writing job applications always consider what skills are required for the job and adapt your CV appropriately.

Some phrases and sentences I could use...

I have managed/supervised...

I have experience working in...

My duties included...

I am responsible for...

This was an exciting and challenging role.

I have a proven ability...

I worked closely with my colleagues to...

This taught me how to...

I have built on...

I am passionate about...

I wish to...

In your PERSONAL STATEMENT...

Ask yourself why you want to study your subject. Then, demonstrate that you have the skills and knowledge to study this subject at university.

PARAGRAPH ONE   *Explain why you want to study your subject.*

Your opening sentence needs to engage the reader ....
For this reason, I find the study of .... to be ....
It is fascinating looking at how ....
I want to study a subject that is challenging and thought provoking, and that always stimulates my intellectual curiosity. (Think outside the box and be original. Show that you are genuinely enthusiastic about studying this subject.)

PARAGRAPH TWO   *Explain how your academic studies, so far, have prepared you to study at university level.*

My academic studies have prepared me to cope with the demands of a .... degree. ....
.... has developed my analytical skills and given me the confidence to ...
.... Likewise, ... has reinforced these skills, teaching me how to .... I have become confident ....
Additionally, ... Throughout my A-levels, I have learnt to balance a heavy workload, manage my time efficiently, and work independently.

PARAGRAPH THREE   *Put down any relevant work experience you have and the skills it has given you.*

My work experience has taught me how to ....
.... This showed me how .... I have been able to put this experience into practice myself, ..., where I am responsible for .... This role has allowed me to develop my interpersonal and communication skills, as well as strengthening how I ....

PARAGRAPH FOUR   *Write about some of your extra curricular activities and the skills you've gained.*

I have accomplished a broad range of activities. I have ....
This taught me how important it is to work in a team. Additionally, ...
.... This improved how I relate to people, and helped me ....
.... A driving force in my life is to .... For example, I took part in .... To achieve this, I had to be extremely self-disciplined and refine my management skills.

CONCLUSION   *Explain concisely exactly why you are suited to study your chosen subject.*

I believe that I have all the qualities and skills needed to study .... I work well under pressure, have excellent communication skills and a good work ethic. A .... degree will be highly rewarding, allowing me to constantly challenge myself.

It is essential that your personal statement is reflective (really thoughtful). Take plenty of time to consider why you want to study your chosen subject and what skills you have.

In your CV...

you need the right words:

Date of Birth: -

Address: 45 Heathervale Road,
Parkland, Surrey,
England, Earth

Nationality: ....

Telephone: 01344 556778

Email: ....

Personal Profile

A conscientious and highly motivated............................... , who can always be relied upon to achieve excellent results and to meet every target set. I have superb communication skills and enjoy working both independently and as part of a team.

Education

....
....
....

Employment History

2008 - Present: ....

Responsible for ....
....
This role has taught me excellent communication skills. I have learnt to adapt easily to new situations.

2006-2008: ....

My main duties included ....
....

Notable Achievements & Interests

....
....

Referees

Use suitable phrases on your covering letter.

5 Cherry Gardens,
London,
WA4

Name and address of business,

Dear Sir or Madam,

I am writing in response to an advertisement I saw in the Daily Herald Newspaper. I would like to apply for the full time or part time position of ……………………………………………………….. I am attaching a copy of my CV for your consideration.

I have gained valuable experience working in ………………………………
………………………….. and have a sound understanding of/ great knowledge of ………………………………………………………………………
In my current position I have acquired good marketing/budgeting/ analytical/ computer/ leadership skills; effectively managing my time so that I meet all my deadlines and targets.

I would be an asset to your organisation and approach the role with enthusiasm. I am hardworking, conscientious and have excellent communication skills. I work well under pressure and am able to deal calmly with stressful and difficult situations. I would greatly value the opportunity to work as part of the team.

Please feel free to contact me via email or phone. I look forward to hearing from you

Yours faithfully,

………………………………

To whom it may concern,

I confirm that .... has been <u>a valuable member of our team</u>. He has shown himself to have <u>remarkable communication skills and the ability to adapt easily to new situations and challenges</u>.

As well as this, I highly recommend him as he has <u>remarkable analytical skills and is full of insightful ideas.</u> He is <u>computer literate, flexible and willing to work on any project.</u> He is <u>highly motivated to learn new skills</u> and <u>consistently achieves good results.</u> Plus, his dedication and commitment helps him meet his targets.

More than this, <u>he has the ability to remain calm in stressful situations and works well under pressure</u>.

I recommend .... as he is: <u>dependable, reliable, hard working, conscientious, courteous and helpful</u>.

He will be an <u>asset</u> ....

Zoggy's Reference

Zoggy can help you use **punctuation** in *your* writing.

Let's get going!

First, don't forget to **write in sentences**. Use **capital letters** and **full stops**.

Jules belongs to **S**ydney at 12 **O**live **G**rove, **R**ushford.

Now try this one:

lois and lulu belong to anya at 14 chesterfield gardens rushford

Use a **!**

That's exciting!
What a surprise!
Oh bother!

Use a **?**

What do guinea pigs eat?

Hold out a piece of vegetable. Will your guinea pig eat it?

Now try this one:

guinea pigs like to be stroked do they bite they are timid but rarely bite ouch

Do not forget to use "**....**" when you use **direct speech,**

"Anya, what did you buy at the pet shop?" said Jules.

"I bought a cage, some straw, some hay, a bowl, a water bottle and some food for my new guinea pigs."

Use commas for **Lists**.

Use commas **before or after** a **phrase** or subordinate **clause** in a sentence.

Use commas **round a clause hidden** in the **middle of a complex sentence**.

Try these:

Lois is lively inquisitive and nosy

Guinea pigs can be chocolate black silver white and tortoise shell.

My guinea pig called Jules has long hair.

After cleaning the cage Anya put in some hay.

Try these: *(answers on next page)*

What is your guinea pig like anya

Lulu has a white coat, uneven coloured spots and black ears she replied

After running in the grass Jules dozed in his hutch.

Guinea Pigs in the wild live in a burrow.

Some guinea pigs with long hair have rosettes.

Use Sounds

ch, sh, wh, th, oo, ee, ar, or, ur, ir, er, e, ai, ay, oi, oy, oa, ow, ou, au, aw, ce, ci, cy, ge, gi, gy, short y, long y, magic e...

... to sound out 80% of words.

Use syllable to sound out hard words.

Eat **VEG ET ABLES**
Soft 'g' - ge, gi, gy.

are **COM FORT ABLE**

like **MIX TURE**

have an **AD VEN TURE**

SEV EN

PRECIOUS

CREATURE

Remember:

1. Sound hard words out using syllables.

2. Jot down words you find difficult. Learn them.

3. Use a dictionary or thesaurus.

Don't forget to keep your writing neat. Small letters should be the same height. There should be one little finger space between each word.

Make sure you can write this passage:

My guinea pigs feed on green leaves. They munch, crunch, scratch, scrunch in their hutch. Early in the morning it is necessary to feed them healthy food and fill up the water container. My noisy young pigs enjoy playing excitedly in their run on the lawn, where they are safe from danger.

Really tricky ones:

'i' before 'e' except after 'c' - when the sound is ee.

believe

fierce

field

conceited

Exceptions:

neighbour

Silent Letters:

Guinea Pigs:

gnaw

clim**b**

eat crum**b**s

are caut**i**ous

are ca**l**m

are **k**nowing

wrinkle up their noses

Tricky words:

Are you **tough enough** to keep a guinea pig?

They can't be **caught**.

They fill one with **laughter**.

They love to be **photographed**.

"Make lists of tricky words you find difficult from the groups of words."

Spelling *Tips* (for guinea pigs!)

"Don't forget it is important to read through your writing, so you can spot any obvious mistakes. Here are a few basic spelling tips. Make sure you can spell all the words on these pages."

Tricky homophones

Homophones sound the same but are spelt differently.

*I gave **two** carrots **to** Jules But he's getting **too** fat.*

***Our** guinea pigs **are** cute.*

*They're over **there** by **their** hutch.*

If the final letter is a consonant, just add the ending.

*He **licks**.
He is **licking**.*

*He **fights**.
He is **fighting**.*

*I **hold** him.
I am **holding** him.*

When you add an ending some words change the 'y' to an 'i':

*My guinea pig is **happy**.
He is **happier**.
He is the **happiest**.*

busy   busier   busiest
cry   cries   cried
piggy   piggies
carry   carries   carried

Difficult Endings

Some words have tricky endings.

*The **latch** on Jules's **hutch** comes open. He gets out and eats a **patch** of grass by the **hedge**. I try to **catch** him but he **dodges** me and runs off.*

*When I **handle** my little piggy, I **cuddle** him.*

Drop the 'e' if you are adding an ending with a vowel.

*I **love** my guinea pig.
I am **loving** him.*

*I **stroke** my guinea pig.
I am **stroking** him.*

*He is having an **adventure**.
He is **adventurous**.*

Use the same rule for:

shine   shiny
noise   noisy

Some words have spelling rules.

You double the final letter of a verb with a short sound.

*I **hug** Jules.
I am **hugging** him.*

*I **pat** the rabbit.
I am **patting** him.*

*I **grab** him.
I am **grabbing** hold of him.*

*He **hops**.
He is **hopping**.*

But, if the ending begins with a consonant you keep the 'e':

live   lively

love   lovely

lone   lonely

safe   safely

	Comparative	Superlative
He is fast.	faster	the fastest
He is fine.	finer	the finest
He is a beauty.	more beautiful	most beautiful

Let's remember **apostrophes**:

The carrot belonging to Jules is **Jule's carrot.**

The hutch of Lois and Lulu is the **guinea pigs' hutch.**

Plus, remember apostrophes for shortened words.

They are gorgeous
They're gorgeous

For extra information you may need to use a **dash** for a longer pause.

Dad bought Anya a guinea pig - it was so sweet.

Jules nibbled his carrot loudly - crunch, crunch, crunch.

Or you could use **brackets** for extra information.

The guinea pigs (Lois and Lulu) scampered across the grass.

Try these:

The guinea pig belongs to Kate.

The hutch of the rabbits George and Ginger.

Isnt he sweet.

Try these:

Anya fed her guinea pig he was hungry.

The rabbits George and Ginger are great friends.

How did you get on?

- Lois and Lulu belong to Anya at 14 Chesterfield Gardens, Rushford.
- Guinea pigs like to be stroked. Do they bite? They are timid but rarely bite. Ouch!
- Lois is lively, inquisitive and nosy.
- Guinea pigs can be chocolate, black, silver, white and tortoise shell.
- My guinea pig, called Jules, has long hair.
- After cleaning the cage, Anya put in some hay.
- "What is your guinea pig like Anya?"
  "Lulu has a white coat, uneven coloured spots and black ears," she replied.
- After running in the grass, Jules dozed in his hutch.
- Guinea pigs, in the wild, live in a burrow.
- Some guinea pigs, with long hair, have rosettes.
- Kate's guinea pig/ the rabbits' hutch/ Isn't he sweet.
- Anya fed her guinea pig - he was hungry.
- The rabbits (George and Ginger) are great friends.
- The male guinea pig is a boar; the female is a sow.

Finally, you can use a **colon** in a list.

Jess had five smart guinea pigs: a short haired coat, a long coarse coat, a deep shining coat, a smooth coat and one with rosettes and twirls.

Or you can use a **semi colon** to separate two similar ideas in a list.

Guinea pigs are sociable; they like company.

Try this:
The male guinea pig is a boar the female is a sow.

Make a sentence with a :
Make a sentence with a ;

More idioms...

Use this page to list any idioms you come across in your day to day life.

Toying with it.
Playing with an idea.

Against the clock
Very busy.

Be my guest
You are welcome

A pain in the neck
a nuisance

Pigs can fly
No chance it will happen

Dead tired
Exhausted

In the way
Your interfering/ not needed

To bear in mind
To remember

No big deal
Not important

Off colour
Not feeling so good

A guinea pig
A person who new ideas are tested on

A little bird told me
I have heard news that

A piece of cake
really easy

Lay someone off
Someone will lose their job

To call it a day
Finish what your doing for the day/ to go home

Behind someone's back
To do or say something, without a person knowing

To be on top of the world
To be extremely happy

A tough cookie
A strong person

www.ingramcontent.com/pod-product-compliance
Lightning Source LLC
Chambersburg PA
CBHW050714090526
44587CB00019B/3368